D1325333

F THE LITTLE BOOK OF red

Rupert Fawcett invented Fred nine years ago
and both their lives have taken off since then.
Rupert has got married and become a father
while Fred has become something of a star with
books and merchandise in several countries.

Fred's past life is documented in Rupert's
eight previous books, *Fred*, *More Fred*,
The Extraordinary World of Fred, *The Continued
Adventures of Fred*, *Carry on Fred*, *At Home
with Fred*, *Pure Fred* and *The One and Only
Fred*. Fred can be seen in the *Mail on Sunday*.

The Little Book of Fred contains sixty-one new
Fred illustrations depicting Fred's strange life
with the good-natured Penelope and ever-
present black cat, Anthony.

First published in 1998
by HEADLINE BOOK PUBLISHING

10 9 8 7 6 5 4 3 2 1

ISBN 0 7472 2197 9

Printed and bound in Italy by
Canale & C. S.p.A

HEADLINE BOOK PUBLISHING
A division of Hodder Headline PLC
338 Euston Road
London NW1 3BH

THE LITTLE BOOK OF
Fred

Rupert Fawcett

HEADLINE

FRED'S LIFE WAS ALWAYS
FULL OF DRAMA

IT WAS SAD BUT TRUE : VERA
REALLY DID HAVE A FACE LIKE
THE BACK OF A BUS

WHILE PENELOPE READ HER GLOSSIES
FRED GOT ON WITH A SPOT
OF GARDENING

PENELOPE FOUND THAT FRED'S NEW
MALE VIRILITY PILL HAD SOME
WORRYING SIDE EFFECTS

FRED WAS BEGINNING TO GET
FED UP WITH PENELOPE'S
VIRTUAL DINNERS

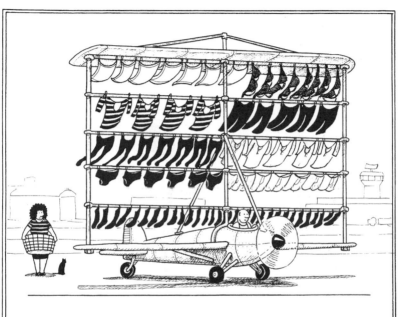

WHEN IT CAME TO DOING THE LAUNDRY
FRED AND PENELOPE MADE
AN EFFICIENT TEAM

APPARENTLY FRED AND THE BURGLAR
HAD BEEN AT SCHOOL TOGETHER

PENELOPE BEGAN EACH DAY WITH
A FEW MINUTES PRAYER AT
HER SHRINE TO GLADYS, THE
PATRON SAINT OF SHOPPING

PENELOPE SEEMED TO TAKE
AGES PUTTING ON HER FACE

'HE'S BEEN LIKE THIS EVER
SINCE HE LOST TINKY-WINKY',
WHISPERED PENELOPE

FRED HAD HIGH HOPES FOR ANTHONY

SUCH WAS THE POWER OF FRED'S
SUPERSTITIOUS BELIEFS THAT HE
REFUSED TO GO ANYWHERE WITHOUT
HIS 'LUCKY' WELSH PINE DRESSER

ANTHONY'S FRIENDS WERE
A CLASSY CROWD

THERE WAS ALWAYS A SMALL PRAYER
BEFORE THE OPENING OF THE
BANK STATEMENT

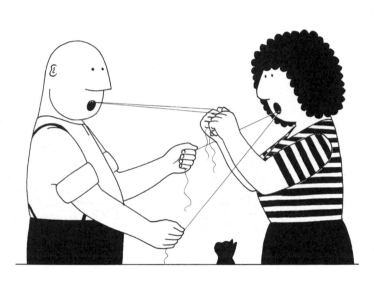

FRED AND PENELOPE LOOKED
FORWARD TO THEIR REGULAR
'FLOSSING' SESSIONS

IT WAS ANOTHER OF PENELOPE'S
TINA TURNER DREAMS

FRED'S SNAIL IMPRESSION SCORED
ONLY A DISAPPOINTING THREE
ON THE CLAPOMETER

AS THEIR NEW LODGER UNPACKED HIS
BELONGINGS FRED AND PENELOPE
BECAME APPREHENSIVE

PENELOPE SOMETIMES WISHED FRED
COULD GET HIMSELF A NORMAL
HOBBY LIKE GOLF OR FISHING

FRED AND PIP WERE NOT
ENTIRELY HAPPY ABOUT THE
LIZ HURLEY INFLUENCE

FRED'S GUESTS WERE EAGER TO SEE
THE NEW 'OPEN-PLAN' GAMES ROOM
HE HAD CREATED IN THE CELLAR

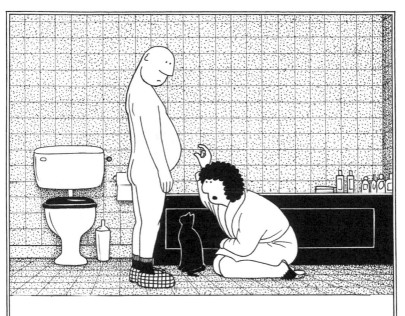

IT WAS SO LONG SINCE FRED HAD
SEEN IT THAT PENELOPE VERY KINDLY
AGREED TO DESCRIBE IT TO HIM

FRED FOUND THAT BY USING AN
INFLATABLE REPLICA HE COULD
POP OUT TO THE PUB WITHOUT
PENELOPE NOTICING HE WAS GONE

FRED'S FRIENDS NEVER TIRED OF
HIS SOFA SWALLOWING TRICK

BY TRAVELLING 'SUPER ECONOMY' FRED
AND PENELOPE WERE ABLE TO AFFORD
A LITTLE HOLIDAY ABROAD

SADLY, DUE TO LACK OF BUSINESS
ANOTHER FRED ENTERPRISE WAS
ABOUT TO GO 'BELLY UP'

'I CAN'T DO A THING WITH HIM',
SIGHED PENELOPE

FRED WAS REWARDED FOR
HAVING HELPED PENELOPE
WITH THE GARDENING

PIP WAS BEGINNING TO WISH HE
HAD NEVER AGREED TO HELP
FRED LAUNCH HIS LATEST
BUSINESS VENTURE

FRED AND PENELOPE FINALLY PERFECTED
AN EFFECTIVE WAY OF KEEPING FIT

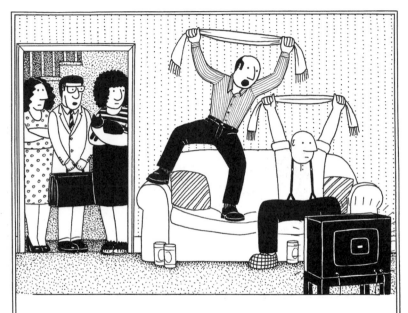

'I'M AFRAID THEY'RE EITHER FOOTBALL
CRAZY OR FOOTBALL MAD,'
WHISPERED THE PSYCHIATRIST

FRED AND PENELOPE LOVED TO TAKE
OFF INTO THE COUNTRYSIDE ON
THEIR EXERCISE BIKES

FRED GENEROUSLY OFFERED TO ASSIST
THE NESBITS WITH THEIR HOUSE MOVE

'I BLAME THE SPICE GIRLS',
WHISPERED FRED

IT TOOK A LOT TO DISTRACT
FRED FROM HIS NEWSPAPER

FRED AND PENELOPE SOON LEARNT
TO IGNORE THEIR LODGERS
FREQUENT PARTIES

FRED HAD NEVER SHARED
PENELOPE'S ENTHUSIASM
FOR SHOPPING

PENELOPE HAD OFTEN HEARD IT SAID
THAT THE WAY TO A MAN'S HEART
WAS THROUGH HIS STOMACH

AT THE TOUCH OF A BUTTON FRED'S
LATEST INVENTION REVEALED
PENELOPE'S INNERMOST THOUGHTS

WHEN FRED HAD FINISHED HIS
IMPRESSIONS THE AUDIENCE
GAVE HIM A BIG HAND

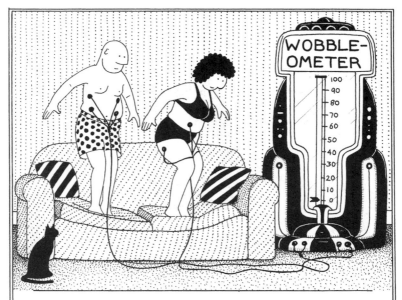

FRED AND PENELOPE FOUND THAT
BY JUMPING FROM THE SOFA THEY
COULD EASILY ACHIEVE A
MAXIMUM SCORE

PENELOPE SEEMED PREPARED
TO GO TO ANY LENGTHS TO
LOSE SOME WEIGHT

SADLY FOR JIM, THE WEARING OF A
TOUPÉE RESULTED IN HIS IMMEDIATE
EXPULSION FROM BLOBB: THE
BRITISH LEAGUE OF BALD BLOKES

AT LAST FRED FOUND PENELOPE
THE PERFECT BIRTHDAY PRESENT

FRED'S STRAP-ON CHAIRS ALLOWED HIS GUESTS TO MOVE FROM THE LOUNGE TO THE DINING TABLE WITHOUT HAVING TO LEAVE THEIR SEATS

AFTER MONTHS OF UNEMPLOYMENT
FRED AND PENELOPE WERE FORCED
TO SELL THEIR HOUSE AND 'DOWNSIZE'

FRED AND PENELOPE REALISED THEY SHOULD HAVE HAD THE CHRISTMAS KISS BEFORE THE CHRISTMAS DINNER

WHILE FRED WAS AT HIS DARTS PRACTICE
PENELOPE DECIDED TO TREAT HERSELF
TO AN INDIAN

JEREMY'S PREDICAMENT CLEARLY
ILLUSTRATED THE DANGER OF
STANDING CLOSE TO TREES FOR
LONG PERIODS OF TIME

PENELOPE COULDN'T HELP FEELING THAT
THE MARKET FOR FRED'S HELICOPTER
SHOES WOULD BE LIMITED

FRED FINALLY DECIDED TO
REPORT THE STALKER

THANKS TO HER PHILOSOPHY AND
THEOLOGY EVENING CLASSES, PENELOPE
HAD FINALLY FOUND THE MEANING OF LIFE

AS PENELOPE OPENED FRED'S CHRISTMAS
PRESENT HE WAS FILLED WITH A
SENSE OF FOREBODING

RELATIONS WITH THE NEIGHBOURS
SEEMED TO BE DETERIORATING

FRED PLANNED TO SPEND THE
MORNING TESTING HIS LATEST
INVENTION : A MOTOR CAR POWERED
ENTIRELY BY NATURAL GAS

FRED AND PENELOPE'S NEWSAGENT
CATERED TO ALL TASTES

'THIS IS THE LAST TIME WE
EMPLOY COWBOY BUILDERS',
RESOLVED FRED

IT WAS A CLASSIC CASE
OF LAWN RAGE

FRED WAS KEEN TO DISCUSS THE
LATEST CREDIT CARD STATEMENT
WITH PENELOPE

AFTER WEEKS OF NEGLECT FRED AND
PENELOPE'S BACK GARDEN HAD BECOME
A BIT OF A JUNGLE

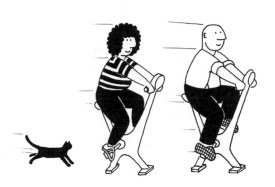